W9-AHC-490

SandCastle™

Signs of the Seasons

SIGNS OF
Autumn

Colleen Dolphin

Consulting Editor,
Diane Craig, M.A./Reading Specialist

A Division of ABDO
ABDO
Publishing Company

visit us at www.abdopublishing.com

Published by ABDO Publishing Company, a division of ABDO, P.O. Box 398166, Minneapolis, Minnesota 55439. Copyright © 2013 by Abdo Consulting Group, Inc. International copyrights reserved in all countries. No part of this book may be reproduced in any form without written permission from the publisher. SandCastle™ is a trademark and logo of ABDO Publishing Company.

Printed in the United States of America, North Mankato, Minnesota
062012
092012

 PRINTED ON RECYCLED PAPER

Editor: Liz Salzmann
Content Developer: Nancy Tuminelly
Cover and Interior Design and Production: Colleen Dolphin, Mighty Media, Inc.
Photo Credits: iStockPhoto/David Winters, Shutterstock

Library of Congress Cataloging-in-Publication Data
Dolphin, Colleen, 1979-
  Signs of autumn / Colleen Dolphin.
    p. cm. -- (Signs of the seasons)
  ISBN 978-1-61783-392-2 (alk. paper)
  1. Autumn--Juvenile literature. 2. Seasons--Juvenile literature. I. Title.
  QB637.7.D65 2013
  508.2--dc23
                      2011051125

SandCastle™ Level: Beginning

SandCastle™ books are created by a team of professional educators, reading specialists, and content developers around five essential components—phonemic awareness, phonics, vocabulary, text comprehension, and fluency—to assist young readers as they develop reading skills and strategies and increase their general knowledge. All books are written, reviewed, and leveled for guided reading, early reading intervention, and Accelerated Reader® programs for use in shared, guided, and independent reading and writing activities to support a balanced approach to literacy instruction. The SandCastle™ series has four levels that correspond to early literacy development. The levels are provided to help teachers and parents select appropriate books for young readers.

Emerging Readers
(no flags)

Beginning Readers
(1 flag)

Transitional Readers
(2 flags)

Fluent Readers
(3 flags)

contents

seasons

There are four seasons during the year. They are called spring, summer, autumn, and winter. The weather, plants, animals, and daylight hours **change** during each season.

autumn

spring

summer

winter

6

autumn

During the year, Earth travels around the sun. This brings some parts of Earth closer to the sun. Other parts of Earth get farther from the sun. Autumn happens in the parts that are moving farther from the sun.

DID YOU KNOW?

In the United States it is autumn in September. In Chile it is autumn in March.

7

It starts to get cold in autumn.
There are more clouds in the sky.
Jordan and Sydney wear their
new yellow hats to stay warm.

There is less daylight in autumn. The sun sets earlier each day. Sarah flies her kite until it gets too dark outside.

DID YOU KNOW?
Autumn is also called *fall*.

During autumn, the leaves
on the trees **change** color.
Then they fall to the ground.

Apples are ready to be eaten in autumn. Ashley helps pick some at an apple **orchard**. Her family goes there every year.

DID YOU KNOW?

Flocks of geese fly in a V-shape.

Geese, ducks, and many other birds fly south in the autumn. They spend the winter in warmer places. This is called *migrating*.

In the autumn, squirrels **collect** nuts. They save them to eat in the winter. It is harder for them to find food in the winter.

DID YOU KNOW?
Autumn comes after summer and before winter.

In autumn, Tristan likes to play in the **crisp**, **crunchy** leaves. What do you do in the autumn?

autumn activities

CARVE A PUMPKIN!

GO CAMPING!

PLAY IN THE LEAVES!

GO ON A HAYRIDE!

22

autumn quiz

Read each sentence below. Then decide if it is true or false.

1. The weather **changes** during each season.
   True or False?

2. There is less daylight in the autumn.
   True or False?

3. Leaves stay the same color in autumn.
   True or False?

4. Geese fly north for the winter.
   True or False?

5. Squirrels **collect** nuts in the autumn.
   True or False?

glossary

change – to be altered or become different.

collect – to pick up or gather things from different places.

crisp – thin and easy to break.

crunchy – making a harsh, crushing sound when pressed or chewed.

migrate – to move from one place to another, usually at about the same time each year.

orchard – a place where fruit or nut trees are grown.